Alexander Wood Inglis, Donald Stuart

The Caledonian Pocket Companion

Being a Collection of the Favourite Scotch Tunes for the German Flute

Alexander Wood Inglis, Donald Stuart

The Caledonian Pocket Companion
Being a Collection of the Favourite Scotch Tunes for the German Flute

ISBN/EAN: 9783337330101

Printed in Europe, USA, Canada, Australia, Japan

Cover: Foto ©ninafisch / pixelio.de

More available books at **www.hansebooks.com**

THE CALEDONIAN POCKET COMPANION

Being a Collection of the most Favourite

SCOTCH TUNES

for the

GERMAN FLUTE

by

James Oswald

VOL

LONDON

Printed for R. Bremner opposite Somerset House Strand.

Caledonian Pocket Companion Vol: II.
INDEX.

A
	Page
At fetting Day	17
Ale Wife and her Barrel	56
Alack and well a day	61
A Highland Battle	68
Annie and Colin	70
A Soldier and a Sailor	74
Armstrong's farewel	75
A Tenant of my own	77
Artless Annie	79
Arthur's Seat	83
A bonny young Lad	84
Annon fide	140

B
Burlesque on Black Joak	18
Birks of Abergeldie	50
Brave Lads of Gallawater	62
Barley Cakes	88
Bonny Sally	100
Black Ey'd Sufan	115
Bohd na Hufudh	117
Bonny laffie take a Man	128
Beware of the Ripples	138
Be conftant still	148
Becaufe I was a bonny Lad	149
Benney fide	156

C
Clout the Caldron	32
Charles Lilt	40
Coming thro' the Broom	ibid
Carron fide	44
Currallans lament	48
Carlands devotion	60
Col: Gardiners lament	91
Crona's Vale	132
Carril's lament	135
Cadger Watty	150
Caftle Swien	151

D
	Page
Deil ftick the Minifter	30
Duncan's Dance	41
Drimen Duff	45
Duncan's lilt	48
Da mihi Manum	50
Duncan's Complaint	85
Drunken magg young	136

E
Earl Douglas lament	30

F
Fairly fhot on her	28
For the Love of Jean	40
Fair Kitty	67
Friendfhip	85
Farewel to Edinburgh	86
Fair Sally lov'd	125

G
Green Sleeves	38
Gentle Love	52
Gallaways lament	53
Gordon Caftle	88
Glenquich's Bufh	109
Gill Morris	147
Goffip Joan	150

H
Hey to the Camp	1
Had I the wate	20
Here awa Willie	39
How fweet it is to Love	66
He til't and fhe til't	73
Hark the Cock crow'd	c
Her Anfwer was Mum	91
Hugar mu Fean	113
Hunt the Squirrel	115
Hark 'tis a Voice	116
Highland King	130
Hi ri ri ri hi	155

Caledonian Pocket Companion Vol: II.

INDEX.

J
	Page
Johnny cock up thy Beaver	2
Jockey was the blitheft Lad	8
Johnny Faa	23
Jenny my blitheft Maid	25
I'll make you be fond	72
Jumping Joan	ibid
Johnny Cope	73
If you had been	80
I have a Wife	90
Jockey's Dream	99
I'll gae nae Mair	101
Juft as I was	114
Jenny's lilt	135
I'll Love no more	137
Jack of the Green	140
Jack Latin	144
Jenny's Joy	146

K
Kittie of Creile	81
Kate of Aberdeen	100
Kick the World before you	101
Secret Dream	106
Kick further	108
Kettle ender	136
Kate of Kinrofs	148

L
Lumps of Pudding	4
Low down in the Broom	6
Lilli Burlaro	13
Lady Barnards Lament	24
Laffie with the yellow Coatie	47
Lude's lament	65
Longoli	70
Lundie's Dream	ibid
Love fick Jockey	78
Lull's Supper	92
Larry Grogan	98
Lauchlan's lilt	102

	Page
Lord Dunmore's delight	111
Laftrumpeny	123
Lona's Vale	138
Lord Antrim's delight	139
Laddie lay near me	143

M
Muirland Willie	11
Mc Pherfon's farewel	14
Mount your Baggage	26
My Love alas is Dead	33
My Love's a bonny naithing	37
My Mother fays I maun not	ibid
Maggie's lamentation	46
Mc Donough's lamentation	50
Matthew Briggs	65
Maggy of Drumlanrig	86
Maid of Allanbank	ibid
Montrofe fcots Meafure	94
Mc Pherfon's farewel	96
Mc Intofh's lament	104
Mc Neil's rant	122
Morfail Lochinalie	124
Mc Duff's fcots Meafure	129
My Appie	ibid

N
Nell of Connaught	84
Norea's wifh	116
Nunc eft bibendum	127

O
Old Sir Simon the King	6
O'er the muir to Maggie	16
Over the Hills	23
Omnia vincit Amor	41
Open the Door to three	61
Oh! Onochie O	66
Ofwald's Complaint	94
One Evening as I loft	99
Ofwald's farewel	130
Ofwald's wifh	134

Caledonian Pocket Companion Vol: II.

INDEX.

Title	Page
Oswald's dream	141
Of all Comforts I miscarry'd	147
P	
Put the Gown	21
Port Athol	45
Peggie of the Green	52
Port Gordon	59
Phillis's Complaint	71
Puries farewel	106
Pioberach mhie Dhonuil	152
Port Patrick	153
Pentland Hills	157
Peggy's Dream	ibid
R	
Ratling roaring Willie	9
Robins Complaint	39
Rory Dall's Port	58
Robin Hood's delight	111
S	
Sailors leads a merry Life	10
Seaton House	13
Symon brodie	42
Scots gavot	44
Saw ye a Lassie	51
Sawney's Pipe	82
Sleepy Maggy	95
Stormont's Ghost	110
Seaforth's farewel	117
Shanbuie	131
St. Patrick's Day	132
She wou'd not die a Maid	158
T	
The old grey Ey'd Morning	1
The Corbey and the Pyett	5
The merry meeting	ibid
The happy Clown	8
Three Sheep skins	10
The Hare in the Corn	12
The auld Maid of Fife	21
The Milk Maid	24
The Maid in the Mill	27
The Scot of Yarrow	28
Thro' the long Muir	30
The Highlanders March	32
The Royal lament	36
The Wars alarms	ibid
The weary pound of Tow	38
The Country Farmer	39
The Widow's lilt	43
The pangs of Love	49
The House under the Hill	51
The Lee rigg	54
The Bride has a bonny thing	55
The Love flip	57
The King of France	60
The Vows of endless Love	61
The bonny wi thing	63
The Battle of Falkirk	64
The malt-man comes on Monday	71
The last Pint Ale	74
The blind Lover	75
The Pot stick	76
The merry Beggers	ibid
There was a Maid	ibid
The Irish Pot stick	77
The Beggars meal Poke	78
The Ivy Buds	ibid
The new Broom	79
The flowers of the Forrest	80
The lovely Lass of Monogon	82
The bell of Craigbidie	83
The Beggers Dance	89
The short Apron	90
The Strathspey Wriggle	93
The small Pin Cushion	94
The drunken Wife	ibid
The Winter it is past	95
The stolen Kiss	ibid

… Caledonian Pocket Companion Vol: II.
INDEX.

Title	Page
The Spinning Wheel	96
The Queen of the May	97
The lucky Minute	98
The birth of Kiffes	99
The cries of Edinburgh	100
The hole in the Riddle	102
The milking Pail	103
The Irish lilt	ibid
The Gimplet	ibid
The Cameronians rant	112
The Voice of my Love	118
This is no my ain Houfe	ibid
The Craiggy Rock	119
The Highland Queen	120
The Banks of Spey	121
The winding of the Stream	122
The Lafs of Leweney	123
The fecret Stream	126
The Widows shall have Spoufes	ibid
The bounding Roe	128
The burfting Sigh	131
The glancing of her Apron	133
The beam of Joy	135
The Maid of Elgin	137
The Scotch Queen	139
The Maid of Forfar	140
The Heither tops	141
The Riel of Harden	ibid
The bonny Lafs of Aberdeen	142
The Shepherd of Neath	145
The bonny Widow	ibid
The brechin Lilt	146
The Hillock of Hay	148
The old Bard	ibid
The lads of Nairn	149
The Sun beam	151
The ferney Bed	152
The Highland fante	154
The Farmer's wifh	ibid
The Lauder's lilt	155
The Thiftle's beard	156
The rifing Breeze	ibid
The Maid of Dornock	ibid
The Leith Scots Meafure	157
The lazy Mift	158
The old Witch of Ochiltree	159
The Vocal fhell	ibid
The Laffie loft	160
The Lafs of the Hill	ibid
The Brides Garter	161
The Man has got	162
The Jeffamine Bower	ibid

U

Up with Aily Aily	25
Urquharts Scots Meafure	45
Under the greenwood Tree	126
Up in a Morning early	143

W

Walley Honey	3
Wallaces lament	7
Woe is me	15
Where will our	22
Was ye at the Bridal	41
When Sol had loof'd	55
What the devil ails you	89
Woo'd and Married and a'	91
Well a day	102
We're a' Kiff'd fleeping	114
What beauteous fcenes	119
Willy's the Lad for me	127
When the King came	133
Wate ye how	134
We'll kifs the World	142
When the Kine	146
Whiftle o'er the leave o't	153

Y

Ye'll au be wellcome	87
Young Colin	93
Yemon O Nock	120

Johnny cock-up thy Beaver

Lumps of Pudding

Brisk

The Happy Clown

Jockie was the Blythiſt Lad in all our Town

Slow

Ratling Roring Willie

Brifk

O er the Muir to Maggie

Slow

Mount my Baggage

Brisk

Here awa Willie

35

Slow

38 Green Sleevs

Brisk

The Weary pound of tow

40 Charles Lilt

Brisk

Coming thro the Broom my Jo.

Slow

Symon Brodie

Moderatly Quick

44 The Scotts Gavot

Carron Side Plentive

The Lafsie with the yellow Coatie

50 The Berks of Abergelde

54 The Lee Rigg

The Ale Wife and her Barrel

Port Gordon

Slow

The Brave Lads of Gallawater

Slow

J'll make you be fond to follow me

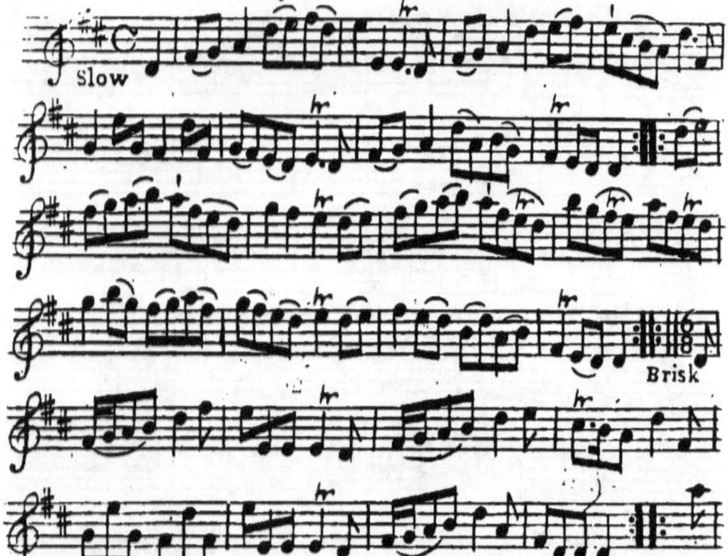

Jumping Joan

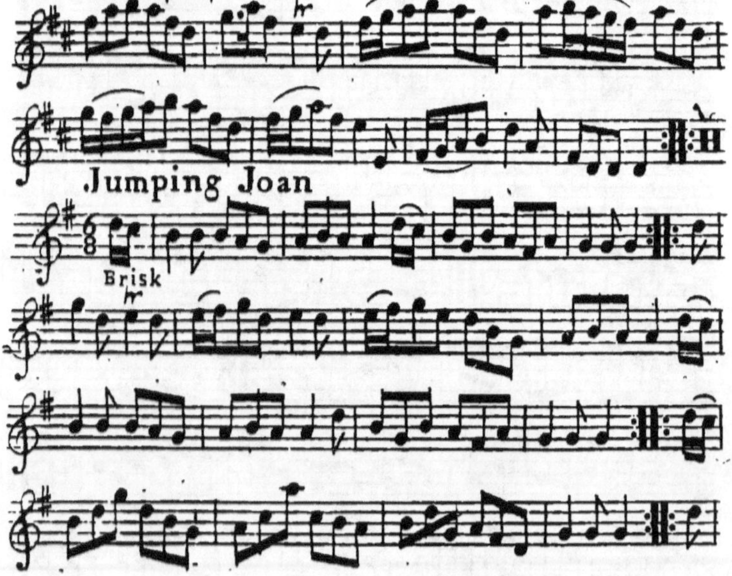

Kittie of Crile

Brisk

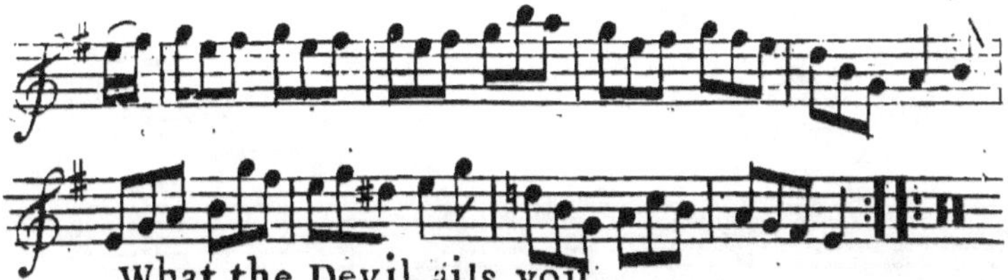

What the Devil ails you

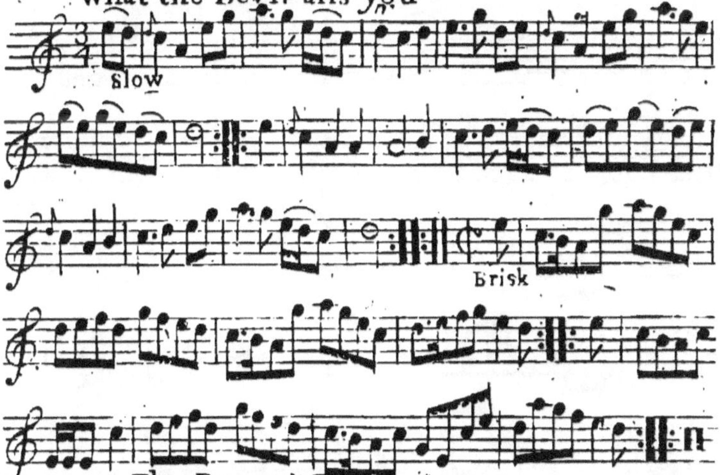

The Beggar's Dance

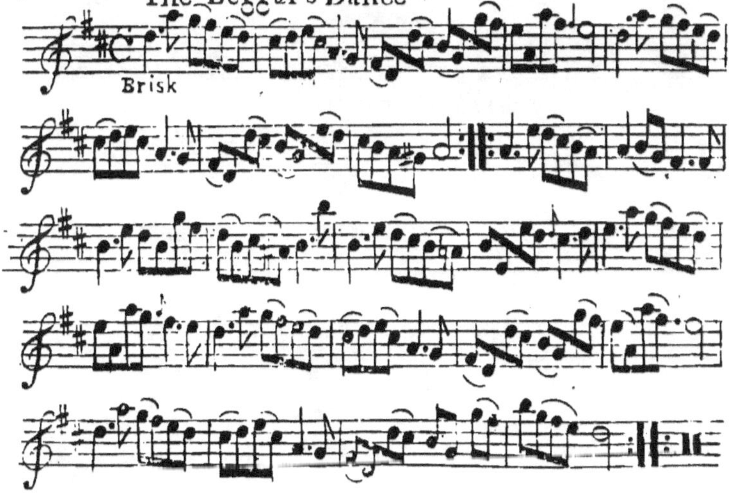

Lude's Supper

96 The Spinning Wheel

Mc Pherson's Farewell

Stormont's Ghost

Lord Dunmore's delight

Moderately Lively

Brisk

Robin Hood's delight

Lively

The Cameronian's Rant

Black Eye'd Susan

Slow

Hunt the squirrel

Lively

What Beauteous Scenes.

Slow

The Craigey Rock

Slow

124
Marſail Lochinalie

(To be begun ſlow and increaſe in quickneſs to the laſt part but one, as the tune repreſents a Battle.

126

Under the Green wood Tree

Brisk

The Secret stream

Slow ... *strong* ... *soft*

The widow's shall have Spouses

Brisk

130 Oswalds Farewell

Plaintive
Slow

Brisk

Highland King
Slow

The Bursting Sigh
Plaintive, Slow

S'hanbuie
Lively

132

Crona's Vale

Slow

St Patrick's Day

Slow

Brisk

Beware of the Ripples

Slow

Brisk

Lona's Vale

Slow

The Scotch Queen

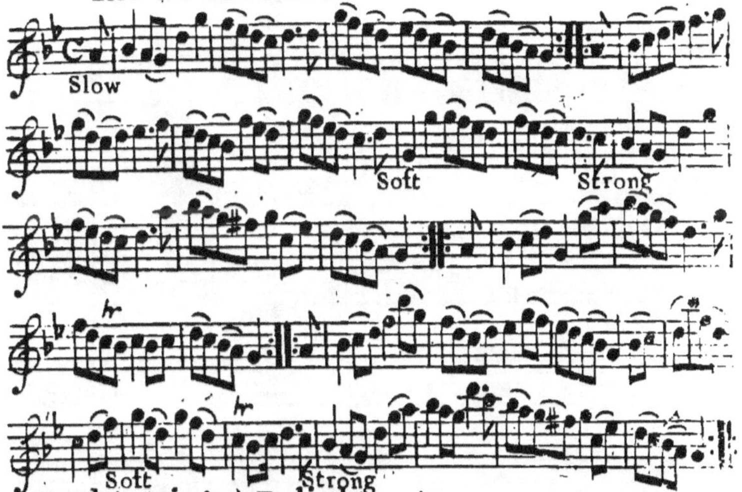

Lord Antrim's Delight

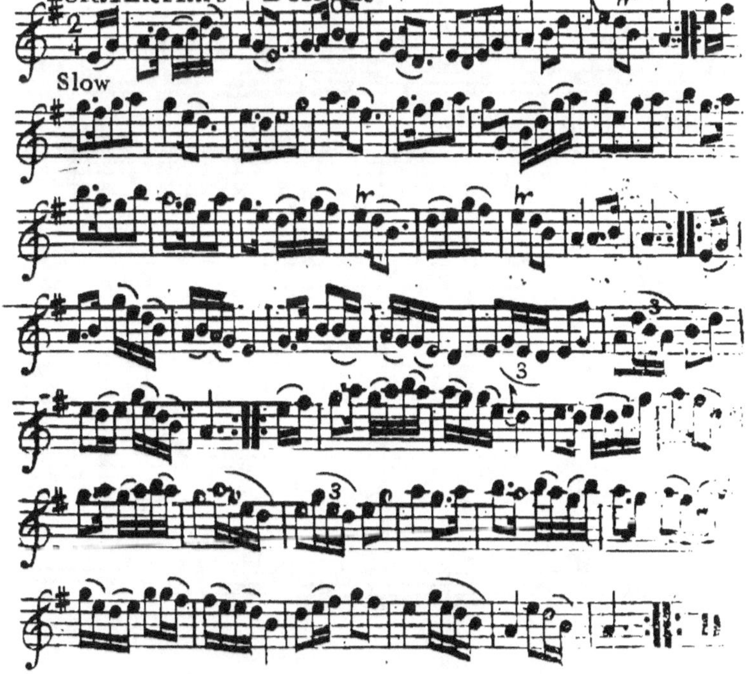

Ofwald's Dream.
Moderatly Lively

The Heither Tops.
Slow

The Reel of Harden.
Brisk.

The Bonny Lass of Aberdeen

Slow

We'll Kiss the world before us

Brisk

144 Jack Latin

Moderately Quick

hen the Kine had given a Pail full

Jenny's Joe

The Brechin Lilt

Of all Comforts J miscarry'd

Gill Morris

Because I was a bonny Lad

Lively

The Lads of Nairn

Brisk

The Highland Sante

The Farmer's Wish

# 162 The Man has got his Mare
The Man has got his Mare again
The Jesamine Bower

www.ingramcontent.com/pod-product-compliance
Lightning Source LLC
Chambersburg PA
CBHW020312170426
43202CB00008B/577